T0339645

A Short Guide to People Management

There is a plethora of information available for busy HR practitioners, but what they really need is a clear, concise and comprehensive analysis of the theory and practice of people management within contemporary organizations. Indeed, much has been written about human resource management (HRM) and organizational behaviour (OB) that rigorously explores each scientific field, yet there is a lack of an integrated examination of both fields.

The author begins by describing the new world of business and management, which is characterized by continuous change and precarious employment. He examines the individual at work, group behaviour, people resourcing, performance and development and the employment relationship, and he concludes with a look at organizational change; that is the nature of the sorts of changes that take place in companies of all sizes and how the process of organizational development can be managed effectively through people management.

This guide provides a thorough examination of the key areas of organizational psychology and people management and offers an easy-to-digest theory on each topic coupled with the latest empirical evidence. All the core theories of HRM and OB are presented in a methodical and critical manner, appealing to time-starved professionals who wish to acquire a detailed overview of people management rapidly. Throughout the book, several suggestions will be made to managers for ways of applying various HR theories to the workplace. The reader will uncover how to manage people but won't be offered prescriptions because the best way of managing people depends on the context.

Antonios Panagiotakopoulos is a Senior Lecturer of Human Resource Management at New York College, Athens, Greece, and a visiting research fellow of the Centre for Employment Relations, Innovation and Change (CERIC), University of Leeds, UK.

Routledge Focus on Business and Management

The fields of business and management have grown exponentially as areas of research and education. This growth presents challenges for readers trying to keep up with the latest important insights. Routledge Focus on Business and Management presents small books on big topics and how they intersect with the world of business.

Individually, each title in the series provides coverage of a key academic topic, whilst collectively, the series forms a comprehensive collection across the business disciplines.

Careers and Talent Management
A critical perspective
Cristina Reis

Management Accounting for Beginners
Nicholas Apostolides

A Short Guide to People Management
For HR and line managers
Antonios Panagiotakopoulos

A Short Guide to People Management

For HR and line managers

Antonios Panagiotakopoulos

Routledge
Taylor & Francis Group

LONDON AND NEW YORK

First published 2016
by Routledge
2 Park Square, Milton Park, Abingdon, Oxon OX14 4RN

and by Routledge
605 Third Avenue, New York, NY 10017

First issued in paperback 2021

Routledge is an imprint of the Taylor & Francis Group, an informa business

British Library Cataloguing in Publication Data
A catalogue record for this book is available from the British Library

Library of Congress Cataloging-in-Publication Data
Names: Panagiotakopoulos, Antonios.
Title: A short guide to people management : for HR and line managers /
    Antonios Panagiotakopoulos.
Description: New York : Routledge, 2016. | Series: Routledge focus on
    business and management | Includes bibliographical references and index.
Identifiers: LCCN 2016008653 | ISBN 9781472478528 (hardback) |
    ISBN 9781315526416 (ebook)
Subjects: LCSH: Personnel management. | Communication in
    organizations. | Organizational change.
Classification: LCC HF5549 .P2443 2016 | DDC 658.3—dc23
LC record available at http://lccn.loc.gov/2016008653

ISBN 13: 978-1-03-209791-6 (pbk)
ISBN 13: 978-1-4724-7852-8 (hbk)

Typeset in Times New Roman
by Apex CoVantage, LLC

Contents

Tables

About the author

Antonios Panagiotakopoulos holds a PhD in Human Resource Management (HRM) from the University of Leeds, United Kingdom, where he serves as a visiting teaching and research fellow at the Centre for Employment Relations, Innovation and Change (CERIC). He is also a freelance senior HR consultant for both large organizations and small and medium-sized enterprises. He has previously worked as a Lecturer in HRM teaching courses at Leeds University Business School and Chester University Business School, as well as a Senior Lecturer of HRM in several higher education institutions in Greece. During his career he has won several teaching and research awards, whilst his articles have been published in various international peer-reviewed academic journals including the *International Journal of Training and Development*, the *Journal of Business Strategy, The Learning Organization* and others.

Acknowledgements

I would like to thank deeply my beloved wife, Nikoletta Mastrogianni, for her endless emotional support during the writing of this book. Also, I extend my thanks to my family, close friends and relatives for their continuous encouragement, as well as to my mentors at CERIC, Professor Mark Stuart and Professor Christopher Forde, for their valuable advice and guidance. Last but not least, I would like to thank Kristina Abbotts at Gower Publishing for believing in this effort from the very first moment.

Introduction

Aims of the book

As the title suggests, this book provides – in an easy-to-digest format – a very comprehensive analysis to the management of people at work for busy HR professionals and other line managers concerned with the management of employees. Essentially, it seeks to outline the purpose and operation of people management (PM) activities in the 'real world' by adopting a critical perspective on the practice of human resource management (HRM). It aims to provide the busy managers with an understanding not only of the potential for HRM to contribute to improved organizational performance and individual well-being at work but also why it very often fails to provide such positive outcomes. The ultimate aim of this book is to raise the awareness of HR and line managers on how to treat their employees as talents and as knowledge users and creators that will drive organizational success.

Significance

Managers of a subject like 'people management', which draws upon several of the social sciences, are likely to be helped by a concise textbook that both gives adequate coverage of the subject matter and maps it out in an accessible manner. The idea throughout the book is to facilitate managers' efforts to match their reading to their daily tasks and to provide them with material to support their people-related activities.

1 Organizations in the changing economy

The purpose of this chapter is to outline the main areas of interest of people management and describe the 'new world' of business and management, which is characterized by continuous change and precarious employment. The role of people management in such a turbulent business environment is also highlighted at the end of this chapter.

People management and organizations

Nowadays, the management of human talents is becoming a prominent component of corporate agendas. It is frequently argued by several commentators from the academia and the business world that intangible people-related assets such as worker skills, relationships with customers and employee involvement in decision-making are becoming more central than ever to organizational success. In this context, it would be surprising – given the degree of organizational restructuring, alterations in the legal context and the attempt to engage the workforce more fully – if people management was not on the organizational agenda to a much greater extent than a decade ago.

However, many employees' experience of employment is shaped by immediate work pressures reflected in concerns about job satisfaction, work intensity and limited discretion. It seems that managers are not addressing effectively the needs and concerns of their workforce in too many workplaces across the world. Although line managers appear to be more sensitive to the significance of HRM than in the past, still this is targeted at providing improved communication rather than translated into tangible improvements in the quality of working life, indicating that people management issues are not sufficiently embedded within mainstream management practice in a large number of workplaces. Therefore, understanding the behaviour of people in organizations is becoming increasingly important as managers' concerns such as staff productivity, quality of work life and job stress start featuring high in their agendas.

There is still little universal agreement on what precisely constitutes HRM, and debates around the meaning of the term still continue. For the purposes of this publication, we will use predominantly the term 'people management' (or PM) instead of 'human resource management' (or HRM), which reflects a humanitarian approach towards managing employees that emphasizes staff commitment, job satisfaction and motivation (as opposed to an instrumental approach that places much emphasis on the quantitative aspects of managing human resources). The working definition of PM that we will use in this book views *people management as the productive management of talents within an organization with the purpose of achieving the firm's strategic objectives and the satisfaction of individual employee needs.*

Two broad models have become particularly influential in the interpretation of people management. On the one hand, contingency-based approaches have developed into strategic HRM to suggest that people management should match with the chosen corporate-level strategy. In particular, the contingency model introduced the concept of strategic PM in which personnel policies are closely linked to the formulation and implementation of strategic corporate objectives. The model emphasizes the necessity of a tight fit between PM strategy and corporate strategy and the use of a set of PM policies and practices that are integrated with each other and with the goals of the organization. On the other hand, what might be termed an absolute position – more is better – has developed around ideas of mutuality and stake-holding at the organizational level. The second influential model, the 'best practice' school of HRM, highlights that there is a universal set of practices (e.g. sophisticated selection, extensive formal training, performance-related pay) aimed at high commitment and high performance that benefit any organization regardless of context. Although both models have some limitations, they have both underpinned the practice of people management so far, with the contingency-based model gaining more support from the available research studies.

The role of HR manager and line managers

The role of HR managers is to undertake certain key activities, including job analysis, labour planning, staff recruitment and selection, workforce skills development, career planning, performance appraisal, compensation and employee relations. As Ulrich stated several years ago, as HRM becomes more business oriented and strategically focused, HR professionals need to become strategic partners, administrative experts, employee champions and change agents. At the end of the day, their core aim should be to make a real contribution to shareholder value.

Line manager action or inaction is often responsible for the difference between espoused HR policies and their enactment. Many HR policies can only be converted to practice by line managers. In so doing, they often reflect the 'informal' culture of the firm rather than the values articulated by top management. Thus, at times, line managers help to keep a sinking ship afloat. At other times, they may be letting a policy die that they think is unworkable or against their interests. Research on managers and their subordinates shows that more effectively developed relationships are beneficial for the individual and work-unit functioning.

One of the essential things that every manager should know when it comes to people management is that great managers try to discover and develop what is different about each person who works for them. Many 'average' managers simply view employees as workers who fill roles; by contrast, exceptional managers view employees as individuals to build roles around. Effective managers are those who try to uncover what is unique in each employee and then capitalize on it. They should value the unique abilities and even eccentricities of individuals and try to integrate them into an HR plan. A manager's time is a very important resource, and great managers should know that the most effective way to invest their time is to figure out how best to incorporate employee idiosyncrasies into the overall corporate plan.

2 People strategy and corporate culture

This chapter aims to explain why modern HRM should be strategic, that is aligned with the organization's general strategy. Also, its purpose is to present the main elements of corporate culture and explain how cultural values and beliefs are created within organizations. The process followed for cultural adaptation will also be explored at the end of the chapter.

Nature of strategy and strategic choices

The meaning of 'strategy' has changed over the last 20 years and become more complex as the literature has moved from emphasizing a long-term planning perspective to a more organic evolutionary process occupying a shorter time frame. Hence, strategic management is seen now to be as much about vision and direction as about planning, mechanisms and structure. Four distinctive approaches to strategy-making have been identified in the literature: the rational-planning approach; the evolutionary approach; the processual approach; and the systemic approach.

The *rational-planning approach* emphasizes a comprehensive analysis of the external and internal environment that then enables the organization to evaluate and from a range of strategic choices that in turn allows for plans to be made to implement the strategy. The *evolutionary approach* suggests that strategy is made through an informal evolutionary process in which managers rely less on top managers to plan and act rationally and more on the markets to secure profit maximization. The *processual approach* recognizes that in practice, strategy formation tends to be fragmented, evolutionary and largely intuitive. While this approach acknowledges the value of the rational-analytical approach, it also identifies the need to take into consideration the psychological, political and behavioural relationships which influence and contribute to strategy. Finally, the *system approach* suggests that strategy is shaped by the social system it operates within. Strategic choices, therefore, are shaped by the cultural and institutional interests of a broader society.

Understanding that strategy formulation does not always occur in a rational, planned manner due to complexities in both the external (e.g. political, economic, social, technological, environmental, legal) and internal environment (e.g. culture, structure) is significant for a manager's understanding of strategic PM.

People and strategy

The early HRM literature appeared to emphasize a strategic theme. However, there was much critical evaluation that demonstrated its lack of strategic integration. The notion of a link between business strategy and the performance of every individual in the organization is central to vertical integration. Vertical integration can be explicitly demonstrated through the linking of a business goal to individual objective setting and to the measurement and rewarding of attainment of that business goal. Vertical integration between business strategy and individual performance is at the core of many strategic HR models. This vertical integration or 'fit' where leverage is gained through procedures, policies and processes is widely acknowledged to be a crucial part of any strategic approach to the management of people and can ensure that competences are created which have a potential to be a key source of competitive advantage. Both vertical integration and horizontal integration (i.e. integration between HR policies themselves) are considered as the essential ingredients that enable the HR paradigm to become strategic.

Just as strategic HRM objectives must be in harmony with the organization's general objectives, HRM activity plans must support the achievement of strategic HRM objectives. For example, an organization that has set cost minimization as its primary corporate objective (i.e. aims to become the cost leader in the market) it would require from the HR department to focus on cost reduction via reduced headcount (i.e. minimal hiring), reduced absenteeism, provision of basic rewards and reduced labour turnover. Similarly, if an organization has set as its core business objective to excel in customer service (i.e. to adopt a differentiation strategy that emphasizes innovation in customer service), this would require the HR department to focus on the selection of highly skilled staff (with an emphasis on employees possessing a range of 'soft' skills), increased formal training provision and generous rewards for top performers.

Organizational culture

Organizational culture sums up the dominant values, visions, perspectives standards and modes of behaviour that typify any one organization. A mature and effective culture will be capable of serving the interests of a full spectrum of stakeholders, including the employees of an organization. The culture-building activities by which a distinctive culture can be developed include the recruitment of like-minded individuals; the development of group norms; the statement of espoused values; the production of mission statements; the introduction of appropriate communication systems; the installation of organizational procedures and rules; the promotion of organizational symbols; the development of key rituals; and the assisting of learning throughout the organization to interpret the founders' vision in practice.

It is evident from the preceding discussion that people management has a central role to play in establishing a unique organizational culture through staff selection, training and compensation that will help an organization achieve sustainable competitive advantage in its markets. For example, the recruitment of employees who are willing to accept the founders' views on how things should be done is vital for developing a distinctive corporate culture. Similarly, training sessions during employee orientation can help a distinctive culture become established. Equally crucial is the role of HR and line managers when it comes to cultural change. As will be discussed more extensively in Chapter 10 of this book, organizational change is not simply a technical matter but a human one. Therefore, when the senior management team decides to introduce a major strategic change, which may involve significant cultural adaptation, the contribution of the HR department is deemed important. For example, the selection of executives and junior staff that espouse the new corporate values along with sufficient in-house training and reward systems are all people-related activities that should be carefully implemented to facilitate the suggested cultural adaptation.

3 The individual at work

This chapter will describe how employees interpret reality and will further investigate the practical implications of perception at work. It will also explore the role that personal values and attitudes play in the way employees perceive various events. Additionally, the concept of personality will be discussed, and its importance for organizational performance will be highlighted.

Values, attitudes, perception

A key feature of every human being is their unique way of looking at things based on their intelligence, their physical abilities and their repertoire of values and attitudes. The concept of 'perception' is very important in understanding human behaviour. In the organizational context, it is how employees interpret the events going on around them that is crucial for the managers. The personal values of individuals along with their perception of social events affect their emotions and subsequently their actions. Most managers struggle to address the 'feelings' of their employees because they ignore that emotions essentially reflect the perceptions held by an individual on a specific issue and that the concept of perception encapsulates a cognitive activity that differs among individuals. A major challenge for managers, therefore, is to try to understand the beliefs held by employees on various issues at work that significantly affect their behaviour. This will help managers enhance employee loyalty and motivation, and it will assist them in taking better decisions during the selection process of new employees.

The most efficient way for managers to learn about employee beliefs is through communication. Managers should make it a priority to walk across the work site and talk to employees in person. Furthermore, they should let employees know from the start that their door is always open. It is important for managers to encourage workers to come to them by creating a safe environment in which employees feel comfortable honestly and openly voicing their frustrations. Without an understanding of individual differences and their effects, managers at work will be considerably impoverished in their roles.

As mentioned in the introductory chapter, people management can be understood as a set of activities aimed at building individual and workforce performance. On the level of individual performance, PM consists of managerial attempts to influence individual ability, motivation and the opportunity to perform. In other words, employees perform when they have:

- *The ability to perform* (i.e. they can do the job because they possess the required knowledge, skills and attitudes). A range of factors can influence an individual's ability to perform a particular role such as their personality, education and previous experience, as well as a number of HR activities including employee training and development.
- *The motivation to perform* (i.e. they will do the job because they feel interested and incentivized). Motivation can be understood both as the individual's choice to perform a particular task and as the level and persistence of effort given to that task. The role of HRM in maximizing employee motivation is to design effective reward systems that involve financial and non-financial incentives to stimulate workers to perform to their potential in a direction desired by the organization.
- *The opportunity to perform* (i.e. they will be able to do the job because their work structure and its environment provides the required support for expression). The opportunity to work effectively is provided by a working environment that offers the necessary support to employees to achieve their potential. This support consists of both the formal and informal structures of the firms, including factors such as the quality of available resources, channels of communication (staff empowerment and involvement in decision-making), job influence and discretion afforded to an employee, sufficient time to complete their tasks and so on.

It becomes clear that if HR and line managers wish to enhance employee performance, they need to influence the above-mentioned variables positively.

Personality and its impact on people behaviour

Psychologists have defined personality as consisting of stable characteristics which explain why a person behaves in a particular way. So, for instance, independence, conscientiousness, agreeableness and self-control would be examples of these personality characteristics. Our sense of self is shaped by our inherited characteristics and by influences in our social environment. The process of growing up – such as the impact of our early family life, the country in which we live – has a significant part to play in our identity. Most social scientists would agree that both inherited and environmental factors are important in our development, and it is the way in which these factors interact which is the key to our adult personality.

Although personality is a powerful determinant of an employee's effectiveness, account must also be taken of the social rules and expectations within the workplace. There is no doubt that in some organizations these expectations are very forceful and insist upon behaviour which conforms to cultural demands. Furthermore, organizations may require different temperaments depending on whether they are going through a period of growth or retrenchment. Whereas an employee may be rewarded for product development in one situation, an employee with other personality characteristics may be needed if the situation changes and there is a period of slow-down and attention to detail and costs.

One of the most widely accepted theories to explain personality differences is the 'big five' concept. According to this theory, the five most consistent traits that are found among individuals are neuroticism (anxious versus calm); extraversion (sociable versus isolated); openness (curious versus incurious); agreeableness (good-natured versus irritable); and conscientiousness (well-organized versus disorganized). Managers need to be aware of such traits since they can be an aid to employee selection and development.

The definition of personality given earlier in the section assumes that personality results in predictable patterns of behaviour, and for this reason the personality concept is significant for organizations. Organizations have their own cultures and accepted patterns of behaviour, which means that some people are likely to fit into a culture better than others. In addition, jobs differ in terms of the personal characteristics they require, and so an individual's personality could have an impact on their suitability for certain roles.

By increasing their awareness on individual personality, HR and line managers can make better decisions during staff selection, they can design suitable training programs, they can provide tailored-made rewards and they can act with greater sensitivity towards employee needs. As mentioned before, the most effective way to understand the characteristic behaviour of any individual at work is through communication and observation. Therefore, managers need to be available to have frequent contact with their subordinates. The importance of communication will also be discussed in Chapter 12.

4 Group behaviour

This chapter will investigate the impact of both formal and informal teams on firm performance and will critically examine the variables affecting team effectiveness, such as the size of the group, the nature of group tasks, team cohesiveness, group norms and so on. The decision-making process within groups will be described, and the problems that often arise in group communication will be explored.

Definition and types of teams

Individuals seldom work in isolation from others. Groups are a characteristic of all social situations and almost everyone in an organization will be a member of one or more groups. Work is a group-based activity, and if the organization is to function effectively, it requires good teamwork. The working of groups and the influence they exert over their membership is an essential feature of human behaviour and of organizational performance. The manager must use groups in order to achieve a high standard of work and improve organizational effectiveness. There are many possible ways of defining what is meant by 'a group'. The essential feature of a group is that its members regard themselves as belonging to the group. Although there is no single, accepted definition, most people will readily understand what constitutes a group. A popular definition defines the group in psychological terms as any number of people who (1) interact with one another; (2) are psychologically aware of one another; and (3) perceive themselves to be a group. Another useful way of defining a work group is a collection of people who share most, if not all, of the following characteristics: a definable membership; group consciousness; a sense of shared purpose; interdependence; interaction; and an ability to act in a unitary manner.

Groups are deliberately planned and created by management as part of the formal organization structure. However, groups will also arise from social processes and the informal organization. The informal organization arises from the interaction of people working within the organization and the development of groups with their own relationships and norms of behaviour, irrespective of those defined within the formal structure. This leads to a major distinction between formal and informal groups.

Informal teams have various advantages and disadvantages. On the one hand, they can enhance the job security of their members since employees feel that they belong to a wider social unit within the firm that can provide them with a strong collective voice; facilitate workforce skills development through the daily interaction of their members (i.e. informal learning); provide significant psychological support since they give the opportunity to their members to share their problems and get advice on various personal and professional issues. On the other hand, informal teams may encourage their members to adopt behaviour that comes in contrast to the key corporate values (e.g. not being punctual at work), which may consequently affect the overall organizational performance.

HR and line managers should know that informal group leadership is likely to be exercised on a charismatic basis rather than by legitimate authority, and power rather than authority is more influential when it comes to informal teams. Also, informal groups generally meet social and security needs before other needs. Given the several benefits of informal teams to individual and organizational performance, it should be among the key roles of managers to facilitate the development of informal teams (through various weekly social events, emphasis on team-working, sports activities after work etc.) but at the same time encourage them to match their aspirations with those of the whole organization.

Improving and measuring team effectiveness

Team effectiveness can be looked at from a number of different perspectives, such as how well the team is fulfilling its overall purpose, how efficiently the team uses its resources, how cohesive the group is, how well the team copes with any difficulties and so on. Some of the steps that line managers can follow to create high-performing teams according to most research studies are the following:

- Set clear and interdependent tasks so team members have to interact with each other in the performance of the tasks (i.e. increasing the frequency of interaction among team members). With wise leadership, this can help team members to learn to trust each other, drawing appropriately on members' skills, and to handle intergroup conflict.

- Set challenging goals, as well as provide clear directions. This enables team members to avoid boredom and reduces employee errors.
- Stimulate individual learning through coaching so as to develop further the knowledge base of team members and enhance collaborative learning.
- Provide team rewards for superior performance, as well as for knowledge sharing. Recognizing team excellence through praise and bonus, for example, can enhance team motivation significantly.
- Hold each member accountable for team performance to prevent 'social loafing' (i.e. the phenomenon where some members exert much less effort than the rest) from occurring.
- Ensure that adequate organizational support is provided in terms of equipment and materials, and provide the team with authority so members can implement their tasks within their allocated time limit.
- Encourage team autonomy to increase members' satisfaction.
- Place emphasis on the size (i.e. large enough to generate flexibility in task allocation but not so large to have problems in communication) and composition of the group (i.e. teams that have members with high level of technical knowledge, score high on the personality dimensions of agreeableness and consciousness and have little demographic diversity are likely to excel). As Meredith Belbin argued several years ago, teams need to consist of individual members who have certain behavioural characteristics that enable them to play nine specific roles. The team roles are the co-ordinator (the person who has a clear view of the team objectives and is skilled at inviting the contribution of team members in achieving these); the shaper (the individual who is full of drive to make things happen and get things going); the plant (the one who is likely to come out with original ideas and challenge the traditional way of thinking); the resource investigator (the group member with the strongest contacts and networks); the implementer (the individual who is effective at turning big ideas into manageable tasks); the team-worker (the person who tries to promote harmony and reduce conflict within the team); the completer (the one who drives the deadlines and makes sure they are achieved); the monitor evaluator (the person who is good at seeing all the available options and can judge situations accurately); and the specialist (the one who provides specialist skills and knowledge around a project).

Line managers should be in a position to evaluate team effectiveness using a list of criteria. The key characteristics of effective and ineffective groups are presented briefly in Table 4.1.

Table 4.1 Examining group effectiveness

Effective groups	Ineffective groups
– Members listen to each other and there is much knowledge sharing – The overall atmosphere is relaxed and harmonious – Ideas are expressed freely – Leadership is shared when appropriate – Conflict is resolved constructively – The group monitors and examines its own progress and behaviour	– Members tend not to listen to each other and the discussions are dominated by a couple of members – The overall atmosphere may be bored or tense – Ideas are suppressed for fear of criticism – The leader retains tight control – Conflicts are either avoided or they destroy members' morale – The group avoids discussing its progress

Decision-making and communication in groups

One of the primary aims of managers should be to achieve group cohesiveness. Group cohesiveness refers to the closeness of a group. A cohesive group has strong bonds that bind the members in loyalty to and support for each other. Team spirit and collaboration are the positive outcomes. However, the negative aspect of increased team cohesiveness is the phenomenon of 'groupthink', as introduced by Janis a few decades ago. Groupthink is a psychological phenomenon that occurs within groups of people where group members try to minimize conflict and reach a consensus decision without critical evaluation of alternative ideas or viewpoints. Managers can limit this phenomenon by giving the power to each team member to evaluate any decisions taken by the team leader; creating smaller teams with different leaders; and having follow-up meetings to review again the initial decisions taken.

One of the major challenges of line managers when it comes to team management is how to manage conflict among team members effectively in order to contribute to organizational effectiveness. The literature has identified so far five main conflict management techniques that line managers can use, which are the following: *the competing style,* where the manager attempts to overwhelm an opponent with formal authority and the use of power (proper when emergency action is required and unpopular actions to employees such as downsizing may need implementation); *the collaborating style,* where the manager attempts to satisfy the concerns of both sides through honest discussion (proper when both sets of concerns are too important to be compromised); *the compromising style,* where the manager strives for partial satisfaction of both parties' desires by seeking a middle ground (proper when opponents with equal power are committed to mutually exclusive goals); *the accommodating style,* where the manager gives in to another's wishes (proper to maintain cooperation when issues are more important to others than yourself); and *the avoiding style,* where the manager attempts to avoid the conflict (proper when an issue is trivial).

5 People resourcing

The purpose of this chapter will be to investigate the process through which organizations attempt to ensure that they have the right number of qualified people, at the right jobs, in the right time. The available techniques used by organizations to forecast labour supply and demand will be discussed along with the most popular recruitment and selection techniques.

People planning

Traditionally human resource planning, generally termed 'manpower planning', was concerned with the numbers of employees and the types of skill in the organization. The emphasis has been on balancing the projected demand for and supply of labour. However, this model appears to be too narrow since it ignores the 'softer' issues of employee behaviour, organization culture and systems. Hence, the framework we will use in this chapter attempts to bring all aspects of HR planning together because these aspects are all critical in terms of programming and achieving the corporate vision.

As part of the strategic planning process, HR planning considers both the internal and external influences on an organization. The first stage of HR planning is situation analysis and environmental scanning. The frequent monitoring of the overall macro-environment (political, economic, social etc.) is necessary to help managers forecast labour demand and external labour supply. This is the point at which HRM and strategic planning interact. The strategic plan must adapt to environmental circumstances and HRM is one of the primary mechanisms that an organization can use during the adaptation process. Examples of external influences that may impact the management of human talent include political attitudes towards unions and management rights; laws regarding hours of work, holidays and compensation; technological advancements that encourage web-based staff training; social values towards minorities; rate of unemployment; and so on. On the other hand, internal influences may involve factors such as organizational culture and structure. The core values of a company impact employee motivation, whereas the organization's structure impacts staff productivity (i.e. organizations with narrow spans of control that are hierarchical in structure tend to be rigid and authoritarian, whilst firms that are flat in structure tend to be more flexible and adaptable). A common mistake for the HR manager is to focus on short-term replacement needs rather than on the firm's long-term people requirements. Such a non-strategic and reactive approach can cause a series of dilemmas for the organization and is inefficient. There are two main approaches in the HR planning activity: the quantitative approach and the qualitative one. Quantitative HR planning uses statistical and mathematical techniques such as trend projection and econometric modelling to forecast HR shortages and surpluses. By contrast, the qualitative approach uses expert opinion (usually the opinion of line managers) to predict the future. In this approach, a panel of experts makes predictions on labour demand and supply using their experience, as well as various sources of information (e.g. governmental reports, research studies on various sectors of economic activity, national statistical data on demographics and education etc.). Two very popular tools that managers can use to predict labour demand and supply are (a) the staff turnover index [i.e. (number of employees leaving the organization during the month ÷ number of employees during the month) × 100], which indicates the rate of people leaving the organization at a given time and (b) the skills inventory, which is a company-maintained record of employees' abilities, skills and education that can be used as a good indicator of the internal labour supply.

In case the supply forecast is less than the demand forecast, then the possibilities are to increase staff training to encourage multitasking; delay staff retirement; reduce staff turnover; use overtime; change the company objectives, as lack of human resources may prevent them from being achieved. On the other hand, when the demand forecast is less than the supply forecast, the possibilities are to consider the costs of over-employment over various timespans; consider the cost of losing staff; consider the costs of staff retraining and redeployment; consider if it is possible for the company objectives to be changed (e.g. move into new markets)

As a concluding comment, it should become clear that two of the key requirements for effective HR planning are (a) a healthy communication between HR and line management and (b) the integration of the HR plan with the organization's strategic plan.

People recruitment

Potential vacancies may occur either through someone leaving the organization or as a result of expansion. Recruiting a new employee may be the most obvious tactic when a vacancy occurs, but it is not necessarily the most appropriate. As mentioned in the preceding section, some of the options that HR and line managers need to consider are the following: re-organize the work; use overtime; mechanise the work; stagger the hours; make the job part-time; subcontract the work; and use an agency.

The final decision will be affected by several factors, including the chosen business strategy of the organization, the nature of the job, the available budget, the prevalent organizational culture and so on. If the decision is that the organization is going to recruit, then a detailed job analysis should be conducted so that an accurate job description and person specification can be produced. Job analysis is the systematic investigation of the tasks and responsibilities of a job and the necessary knowledge a person needs to have to perform the job adequately. Job analysis is normally conducted by HR managers or line managers. In particular, HR managers collect information about job content and the personal requirements needed to do the job successfully, usually through observation of the job holder or/and interviews and questionnaires with the job holder. The final outcome is the development of job descriptions. The personal requirements that individuals need to have are usually called competency characteristics, and they normally involve motives, traits, values, knowledge and skills (both *hard* skills such as IT skills and other technical abilities and *soft* skills such as empathy, creativity, persuasiveness etc.).

Job descriptions and person specifications normally involve the job title and context (e.g. location, information about the company); the job summary (e.g. duties, working conditions, performance standards); and the required, as well as desirable, attributes needed by the individual to perform successfully in the job. It should be noted that although job descriptions are important organizational documents that guide decision-making of HR managers during recruitment and selection, they have been criticized for being a static written description of a job, ignoring its dynamics. Therefore, nowadays, job descriptions should be as flexible as possible.

During recruitment and selection, managers need to be careful so as not to discriminate against potential employees on the basis of unrelated job characteristics including gender, age, disability, ethnicity, sexual orientation, religious beliefs and so on. This is important not only for legal and ethical reasons but also for economic reasons since managers may lose valuable talent if they discriminate against future employees. For example, several research studies have revealed that people with disabilities, if matched to the right job, are very productive and loyal to their organizations (in some cases, they are even more productive and committed to organizational objectives than employees with no disabilities). Similarly, research indicates that older workers can be more reliable than younger workers and can have a greater ability to handle complex issues.

The available recruitment techniques can be divided into two main categories depending on whether the organization fills the vacancies internally (i.e. using existing employees) or externally (i.e. using candidates from the external labour market). The most popular techniques are presented in Table 5.1. All the various techniques have benefits and drawbacks, and the choice of a technique has to be made in relation to the particular vacancy, the type of labour market in which the job falls and the organizational objectives. Additionally, the HR and line managers need to take into account the main advantages and disadvantages of internal and external recruitment, which are summarized in Table 5.2, in order to reach a final decision on how to fill any job vacancies.

Table 5.1 Internal and external recruitment techniques

Internal recruitment	External recruitment
– Announcement of job vacancies using the company's intranet – Newsletter – Bulletin board – Word of mouth	– Advertising through Internet, radio/ TV, local press, corporate website, magazines – Employment agencies – University recruiting/career days – Employee referral scheme – Posters – Unsolicited applications

Table 5.2 Strengths and weaknesses of internal and external recruitment

	Advantages	Disadvantages
Internal recruitment	– The candidate is familiar with the organizational culture, so induction training is kept to the minimum – Managers have already evaluated the candidate's work performance – Employee motivation is enhanced since staff understands that the company cares about employee development – It is normally less time-consuming since no extensive advertisement is needed	– Employee infighting for promotion may affect staff morale – Employees may get promoted beyond their level of competence (due to social networking inside the company)
External recruitment	– The pool of candidates is greater – Fresh ideas may be brought into the company from newcomers who have worked in different corporate environments	– More initial training is required to help newcomers become familiar with some basic organizational norms

Evaluation of staff recruitment

The last part of the recruitment process should involve an evaluation stage to identify the strengths and weaknesses of the firm's recruitment process. In order to evaluate the effectiveness of their recruitment practices, HR managers need to use the following four main criteria:

- *Productivity of the selected recruitment technique.* This concerns the number of applicants generated by each recruitment method
- *Quality of applicants.* This is about employee performance ratings by recruiting method.
- *Cost.* This involves the total cost per applicant per recruiting method.
- *Time.* This criterion concerns the applicant response time per recruitment method.

People selection

After the recruitment process, there is the short-listing process where the HR manager needs to identify the candidates most likely to perform successfully in the job. During that process, managers need to look at the essential and desirable skills and attributes of the individual candidates, assigning the candidates scores against each item in the list of criteria. Managers can then record the scores on their spreadsheet and rank the candidates.

It is quite unusual for one selection method to be used alone. A combination of two or more methods should generally be used to strengthen the validity of the selection decision. The choice of the methods is dependent on various factors, including the selection criteria for the post to be filled, the abilities of the HR manager, administrative ease, time factors and cost. Various selection techniques are available – including interviews (e.g. face-to-face, telephone, video), tests (e.g. intelligent tests, personality tests), trial days (employees spend some days on a probationary basis), references from previous employers and medical tests – with the most popular being discussed in the next sections.

Interviews

Interviewing continues to be the most popular selection method. It is a planned conversation with a purpose of gathering rich data about an individual. The format can include biographical data, as well as information on the key competencies of the individual and aspects of his or her personality. Over the years, interviews have received relatively bad press as being overly subjective, prone to interviewer bias and therefore unreliable predictors of future performance. Such criticisms are levelled specifically at unstructured interviews, where the interaction is not standardized. In response to this, developments have focused on more formally structuring the interview or supplementing the interview with less subjective selection tools such as psychometric tests and work sampling. However, interviews can provide the HR and line managers with lots of information on the individual's skills and personality. In particular, the HR manager can observe the body language of candidates and determine if they have the necessary social skills, motives and traits required for the job (considered to be the hidden individual abilities); assess the candidate's job knowledge; and evaluate if the candidate fits with the overall team and corporate culture. Arguably, the main disadvantage of interviews is the interviewer's bias (since it is based on subjective evaluations that are affected by variables such as gender, age, previous experience etc.) that may affect their final decision. That is why it is recommended that at least three interviewers be present during the selection process, including the HR manager, the line manager and an experienced colleague.

How to conduct interviews effectively

The following steps should be followed by HR and line managers in order to conduct effective interviews:

1   They should know the job very well. This means that they need to be very familiar with the job context, personal attributes and skills required for the vacancy to be filled.
2   They should set specific interview objectives (i.e. what information they wish to get) prior to the interview.
3   They need to provide the proper setting for the interview (i.e. quiet environment free from interruptions).
4   They should review the applicant's CV prior to the interview to determine what additional information is required and also to show the applicant that they take him or her seriously (i.e. that managers have spent time looking at applications instead of reviewing the application for the first time during the interview!).
5   They should beware of their prejudices. Almost all managers have prejudices of some sort, and hence, they need to recognize them and challenge them. If applicants are to be evaluated objectively, managers' stereotypes should not impinge on the selection decision; otherwise the organization may lose some very talented candidates.
6   They should not make snap decisions. Research shows that most interviewers make a judgement about an applicant in the first 5 to 10 minutes of the interview, and from that point on, they 'hear' only information

that confirms their initial impressions. However, this is a wrong tactic since reliance on stereotypes normally diminishes as more information becomes available to the interviewers. As a golden rule, what managers need to know is that judgements should be reserved until all relevant information has been gathered.

7 They should pay much attention to the body language since it may reveal what the applicant is really thinking or feeling. Most non-verbal signals usually stem from the unconscious, and as such they can be very accurate indicators an individual's thoughts.

8 They should encourage the applicant to do most of the talking through frequent 'probing' instead of using the interview as a means to promote the overall image of the organization itself. Managers should not forget that the core purpose of a job interview is to learn as much as they can about the applicant. The interviewer should not monopolize the discussion talking about himself or herself. The employment interview should be considered as an important business meeting and not as an opportunity for the manager to share their favourite stories with the applicants.

9 They should explain the nature of the job to the applicant so that he or she is fully aware of the tasks and responsibilities associated with the post.

10 They should close the interview in a very polite way, write up the interview soon after (i.e. full transcript) and evaluate the interview. Accuracy is increased if facts and impressions are recorded as soon as possible.

List of 15 key questions to be asked during a job interview

1 What motivates you the most?
2 What brings you joy at work?
3 What kind of responsibilities would you like to avoid in your next job?
4 What job was the most frustrating and why? How did you remain motivated to complete it?
5 What kinds of people would you rather not work with?
6 Have you ever had to resolve a conflict with a colleague or client? How did you resolve it?
7 Tell me about an objective in your last job that you failed to meet and why. What have you learned from your mistakes?
8 Describe a situation in which you had to take a risk.
9 Describe a situation in which you had a difficult problem at work. How did you solve it?
10 Tell be about the best/worst boss you ever had. What made it tough to work for him or her?
11 Describe some situations in which you worked under pressure.
12 Give me an example of when someone brought you a new idea, particularly one that was odd. What did you do?
13 Can you describe for me the last time you 'broke the rules'?

14 How do you measure your own success?

15 What do you expect to find in our company that you don't have now?

Tests

Tests have been used for selection purposes for several decades, but there has been a significant rise in test use over the last decade as the selection process has become more sophisticated and rigorous. The types of tests used more frequently are ability and aptitude tests, intelligence tests and personality tests. Tests offer various benefits to managers, including information on the personality type of an employee (e.g. tests can identify interpersonal traits that may be needed in certain jobs). However, their validity has been questioned mainly due to the fact that they are static and ignore several contextual variables that may affect performance at work (e.g. support from colleagues, quality of supervision etc.).

Tests must be chosen with care by HR and line managers. There are some specific characteristics of a 'good' test:

- It should be a sensitive measuring instrument, which avoids discriminating between subjects.
- It should be standardized on a representative and sizeable sample of the population for which it is intended so that any individual's score can be interpreted in relation to others.
- It should be reliable in the sense that it should always measure the same thing when applied to different people at the same time or to the same people at different times.
- It should be valid in the sense that it should measure the characteristic which it is planned to measure.

Evaluation of staff selection

The last part of the selection process should involve the evaluation phase. Three main criteria can be used by managers to evaluate their staff selection practices:

1 *Quality of selection method.* This can be decided using employee performance ratings (i.e. during performance appraisal) per selection method. The performance of each employee is evaluated against certain criteria and then matched with the selection method used for each applicant.

2 *Time.* This criterion concerns the time spent per selection method to choose the most suitable applicant.

3 *Cost per selection method.* This involves all the expenses incurred per selection technique to determine the cost-effectiveness of each selection tool.

6 Measuring people performance

The purpose of this chapter would be to discuss the relationship between corporate strategy and performance appraisal (PA). The major types of performance appraisal systems will be explored along with their strengths and weaknesses. Also, the sources of error in performance appraisal will be discussed.

Performance appraisal

Traditionally, performance appraisal systems have provided a formalized process to review employee performance. They are usually centrally designed by the HR function, requiring each line manager to evaluate the performance of their staff throughout the year. This normally requires the manager and employee to take part in a performance review meeting. What is being appraised varies and might cover personality, behaviour or job performance with measures being either quantitative or qualitative.

By providing a dynamic link to employee recruitment and selection, training and development, compensation and employee relations, PA is a vital tool for strategy execution. It signals to managers and employees what is really important, it provides ways to measure what is important and it helps to improve performance. It is also a necessary activity to defend line managers against employees who challenge the validity of management decisions relating to promotion, transfers, salary changes and termination.

An essential component in setting realistic targets and reviewing prior performance is the ability to measure job performance in an objective manner (as far as this is possible). Setting appropriate measures of performance is essential for providing useful feedback, allowing areas of positive performance to be further developed and areas of poor performance to be addressed through corrective action. There are two broad approaches to performance measurement. The first is focused on results or outputs where performance can be quantified and metrics used to determine the achievement of objectives (e.g. sales targets). The second approach involves the grading of performance levels where performance cannot be measured in quantitative terms. This is useful when assessing the behavioural aspects of performance. This latter approach is gaining in importance as managers place greater emphasis on the kind of behaviour they want their employees to exhibit and the process by which desired objectives are achieved. Arguably, both goals and behaviours should be considered when evaluating job performance to guard against undesirable employee behaviour in the achievement of objectives.

The stages in a performance evaluation system start with the definition of business role (i.e. creation of job description and objectives of department). The organization should have made significant steps in identifying the performance required of the organization as a whole. This will involve a mission statement, strategic objectives and job descriptions. These objectives along with the agreed job descriptions should be tightly defined and include measures to be assessed. Ongoing coaching during the tasks is important as managers guide employees through discussion and through constructive feedback. Regular formal reviews are needed to concentrate on developmental issues and to motivate the employee. Many systems include a link with pay. Performance evaluation needs to be line driven rather than HR driven, and therefore mechanisms need to be found to make this happen. The incorporation of line managers alongside HR managers in a working party to develop the system is clearly important as it not only takes account of the needs of the line in the system design, but also demonstrates that the system is line led.

At an operational level, there are a number of potential pitfalls in PA, including a failure to gain the support of line managers, inadequate training for line managers in conducting PA, a failure to invest in training initiatives to support performance improvements or a failure to identify and apply appropriate measures of performance. At a more strategic level, overly rigid and bureaucratic PA systems in which goals are too narrow or inflexible and in which there is too great a focus on short-term achievement can lead to the system becoming an inhibitor of change rather than a force for employee motivation and continuous improvement. This can also be the case where the focus on collecting and reporting performance data takes primacy over those activities that actually contribute added value, such as effective employee communication and better workplace relations.

Tools for measuring staff performance

The evaluation of performance is normally done by the immediate supervisor. However, there can be other raters of employee performance, including colleagues, customers and employees themselves. Common rater errors may result from leniency, strictness, bias, prejudice and relationship effect (i.e. quality of relationship between the manager and employees). The major tools of performance appraisal include *ranking* (the manager ranks each employee in order from best to worst); *grading* (employees' performance is matched with a specific grade definition such as superior, good, acceptable, unsatisfactory); *graphic scales* (rating scale that evaluates employee performance using specific employee characteristics such as reliability, quantity of output etc.); *critical incidents* (examples of employee behaviour that illustrate effective or ineffective job performance); *behaviourally anchored rating scales* (BARS) (a tool that combines elements of the traditional rating scale and critical incidents method); *essay description* (a written statement describing an employee's strengths, weaknesses, past performance and future development prepared by the rater); and *management by objectives* (involves setting measurable goals with each employee and then reviewing the progress made).

Arguably, BARS is one of the methods that can offer much detailed information to the job holder around his or her performance and can reduce subjectivity. This tool is designed to evaluate behaviour demonstrated in performing a particular job within the organization. Profiles of good and bad performance in a particular job are collected from supervisors, and these examples are then grouped into various job dimensions such as job knowledge, customer relations, safety and so on. Next, specific examples of job behaviour are placed on a scale, which is usually graded from 1 to 5. A typical example is given in Table 6.1.

Table 6.1 BARS for a training and development officer

Grade	Description of performance
Superior performance (5)	The employee is developing, implementing and refining training interventions to the highest professional standard at all times.
Very good performance (4)	The employee is being proactive and accurate in identifying staff training needs, designing thorough training programs and evaluating them.
Good performance (3)	The employee is arranging holistic training interventions when problems arise.
Satisfactory/Marginal/ Acceptable performance (2)	The employee is showing a basic interest in workforce skills development and possesses only basic knowledge around human resource development.
Poor/Unsatisfactory performance (1)	The employee is showing very little interest in staff development and has very limited knowledge on how the systematic training process works.

It has been found by several research studies that BARS reduces bias during staff evaluation because the positions along the scale are defined in terms of job behaviour. In addition, there is some evidence that employees are more satisfied and committed than those subject to other types of performance evaluation methods. However, BARS comes with some drawbacks including the time and effort taken to develop by HR or line managers. Despite such limitations, it is important for HR and line managers to acknowledge that spending time in developing accurate staff evaluation methods can be considered as an investment, which will result in long-term benefits for the organization given that staff evaluation is closely linked to staff selection and development.

Feedback provision in the performance appraisal process

Dealing with poor performance should be one of the main tasks of HR and line managers. Effective diagnosis requires managers to be prepared to acknowledge their role in employee underperformance and avoid making snap judgements about its root cause. It also requires employees to be candid in identifying problems even where they fear the consequences. If the diagnosis suggests incapability, then learning and development interventions or redeployment to another position should be considered.

The formal performance review meeting is a very important discussion where the manager and subordinate mutually review the employee's job responsibilities, performance improvement and career goals. The performance appraisal interview should be a positive experience for the manager and the employee. Yet, research evidence suggests that very frequently it becomes a stressful and unpleasant activity owing to insufficient manager preparation, lack of training in conducting a job performance review and lack of management commitment towards staff evaluation that may lead to a failure to provide objective feedback. The following are some of the key steps that managers should follow in order to conduct an effective performance review meeting:

- Before the review meeting, the line manager (or the HR manager) should check the employee's performance against the mutually agreed goals and ensure that the entire performance (not just negative factors but positive ones as well) has been considered. Furthermore, the manager should review the employee's job description to make sure that it remains accurate and that nothing has been overlooked.
- During the review meeting, the manager has to describe events, not judging employee performance. The manager should also be constructive,

not destructive, because offensive criticism makes the employee defensive and has a negative effect on goal achievement. In the same line of thinking, focusing on isolated incidents should be kept to a minimum.

- The manager should provide positive feedback in addition to areas for improvement. The review meeting is not supposed to be a discussion where the manager is simply passing judgement. Managers should remember that the discussion must bring mutual benefits. This means that employees should not leave the room angry and demotivated.

- The review meeting must be job behaviour-oriented rather than trait-oriented. The manager should discuss things that can be changed and tolerate some employee weaknesses if those weaknesses do not hinder performance.

- The employee should be encouraged to talk and explain his or her behaviour. Research evidence indicates that the more employees are allowed to participate, the more satisfied they feel with the appraisal discussion. Some typical questions that managers can use to bring the employee into discussion are: What can I do to help you do your job better? How do you feel about your current responsibilities? What training do you think you may need?

- Specific performance improvement objectives should be set (e.g. try to increase the number of calls you receive for customer complaints by 10 percent per week). General and vague targets should be avoided (e.g. you can try a bit more).

- The manager should avoid using positional authority. The discussion should be done in a climate of joint problem-solving and not in an atmosphere where the manager looks forward to judge their staff.

7 People learning

The key aim of Chapter 7 is to outline the importance of human resource development to organizational success. The main principles of learning psychology will be discussed along with the systematic approach to employee training and development. More specifically, the main stages of the systematic approach towards staff learning will be explored followed by a critical analysis of the practices that can enhance organizational learning at work. In short, this chapter will consider how employees learn at work and will identify managerial practices that can facilitate individual learning.

Individual learning at work

Learning is a process by which people acquire knowledge and skills and apply them to solve problems throughout their daily life. Learning involves change of behaviour, which is normally of a relatively permanent kind. Learning is not an automatic process; it is a rather complex process affected by a host array of factors including external factors (e.g. the learning content, the trainer, facilities, rewards) and internal factors (e.g. perception, abilities, motivation, emotions) that all managers should be aware of in order to enhance the learning process. Learning can be undertaken deliberately when individuals consciously 'learn' and 'study'; at such times they will subject themselves to assessments to gauge the level and depth of their understanding and skills. However, much of what we have learned takes place without any necessary deliberations nor any assessments. Learning can be seen to be a continuous and automatic process, often taking place in a social context.

In this section we will explain how individuals learn based on the learning cycle developed by David Kolb. The learning cycle reveals that learning is a continuous process, the direction of learning is determined by individuals' needs and goals and it is affected by different styles of learning.

The learning cycle consists of four main stages. There is the initial stimulus to the learning process (e.g. a damage in the printer or a problem-solving exercise). The experience is then followed by the individual's effort to clarify the problem. This stage leads to the crucial cognitive/thinking stage where the individual attempts to puzzle the problem out and draw conclusions. At a final stage, these conclusions are put to the test. It is important for managers to know that individuals have different learning styles. There are employees who learn through active experimentation, and employees who are abstract thinkers and are keen to develop theoretical models.

The psychology of learning provides some important principles for line managers concerned with delivering effective training. The learning principles are the guidelines to the ways in which people learn most effectively. The more these principles are taken into account in the training process, the more effective training is likely to be. The main learning principles involve:

1   *Participation.* Learning is quicker and lasts more when the learner is actively participating in the learning process. As an old Chinese proverb says, 'I hear, I forget – I see, I remember – I do, I understand'.
2   *Repetition.* Repeating the events or ideas in a learning process facilitates learning. The goal of training is to ensure that desired behaviour occurs consistently, and this can happen when trainees are able to practice and repeat the learning content.
3   *Relevance.* Adult trainees learn more easily when they know that the material which they will be taught is meaningful to them. Otherwise, they will not be motivated to learn.
4   *Transference.* The lesser the gap between training situation and the job, the greater the possibility of knowledge transfer. If employees are not able to transfer their training to the work situation because they are not able to remember all the training information, then the training effort may have been wasted.
5   *Feedback.* Learners need to know about their progress in order to adjust their behaviour and improve their skills to meet the desirable performance targets. Without feedback, there is no basis for a change in behaviour.

Systematic training model

Whatever the format of the training models, they all have individual variations around three main stages: the needs analysis, the implementation and the evaluation phase. Each phase of the process is vital for the design and delivery of a successful formal training program by line managers.

The assessment phase

Needs assessment is a process by which an organization's human resource training and development needs are identified and translated into training objectives. Training needs analysis is partly concerned with defining the gap between what is happening and what should happen. This is what has to be filled by training, that is the difference between what people know and can do and what they should know and be able to do to achieve the organization's goals.

The needs assessment phase provides direction and purpose for the training effort. However, more frequently than enough, training programs get their start in many organizations simply because the program was well advertised and marketed or because other organizations are using it. This means that despite the importance of a needs analysis, many line managers do not perform one, mainly due to time constraints and incorrect manager assumptions that a needs assessment is unnecessary and that the implementation of training is more important. Nevertheless, the needs assessment phase must be the starting point of every training and development process because it can identify gaps between employees' existing skills and the skills required to perform their jobs; gaps between employees' existing skills and the skills needed to perform their jobs in the future; and an organization's goals and its effectiveness in reaching these goals.

In other words, the needs assessment phase establishes what training is needed, by whom, when and where. Without determining the need for training, there is no guarantee that the right training will be provided for the right trainees. Training needs assessment can also reveal if training is the appropriate solution to a performance problem, since all performance issues are not training issues. Other resources such as machines, factory space, methods of work and office utilization can impact work performance and may not have any training implication at all. Finally, it should be noted that the needs assessment phase can be used also as a diagnostic tool since it may reveal shortcomings that can be traced to other human resource activities. Inappropriate placement, selection or recruiting may lead to employees with deficiencies and errors in these activities may stem from faulty human resource planning, job designs and so on.

To ensure an effective training and development program, needs must be measured considering the organization, the job/task, the individual and specific populations of the workforce. Therefore, there are four levels of needs analysis: *Organizational analysis, job or task analysis, person analysis* and *demographic analysis*. Each of the these levels is discussed in the next sections.

Organizational analysis

Organizational analysis (or strategic analysis) is a process used to better understand the characteristics of the organization to determine in which parts of the organization training and development activities should be conducted, where they will be useful and under what conditions they will occur. An organizational analysis should identify organizational goals (i.e. the areas that the organization met its goals and obviously do not require training efforts), organizational resources (i.e. the amount of money available is a significant factor which affects the training and development efforts), organizational climate (i.e. mutual trust as well as cooperation between managers and employees is essential for the success of a training and development program) and environmental constraints (i.e. legal, social, political and economic issues faced by the organization may determine the content of the training programs). Each of these factors provides valuable information for planning and conducting training and development programs. The main tools that can be used by line managers for organizational analysis include manpower inventories, skills inventories, efficiency indexes, organizational climate measures and exit interviews that line managers could use to gather the relevant information.

Task analysis

Job or task analysis (sometimes called operations analysis) is a process of data collection about a specific job in order to identify job performance standards and the knowledge, skills and abilities needed to perform these tasks. The information that should be gathered after a task analysis must include the standards of performance, how tasks should be performed to meet these standards and the skills necessary to perform these tasks. The most common methods available for a task analysis include job descriptions, job qualifications/specifications and performance standards.

Person analysis

Person analysis is concerned with how an employee performs job tasks and how well the employee demonstrates the skills and abilities required by the specific job. The aim of person analysis is to identify the training needs of the individual. Immediate supervisors play a particular important role in person analysis by implementing properly many methods of person assessment. However, it is also possible to be followed a multi-source evaluation approach which involves an individual being evaluated by their superiors, peers, subordinates and customers (360-degree performance appraisal).

The most common methods available for person needs assessment involve performance data, interviews, questionnaires, attitude surveys, supervisor observations and tests.

Demographic analysis

Demographic analysis concerns the different training and development needs that may have specific populations of workers within an organization. This is also an important level of needs analysis since different groups within an organization (e.g. minorities, men and women, low-level personnel and top-level executives etc.) have different training and development needs. For example, first-line employees need training which emphasizes the acquisition of technical knowledge and skills, while top-level executives need training which emphasizes the acquisition of knowledge that helps them form strategic decisions since they are responsible for the direction and scope of an organization over the long term. The data collection methods available for demographic analysis involve mainly manpower inventories.

The implementation phase

The training and development methods available for the delivery of the training program can be divided in three main categories: on-the-job, off-the-job and a combination of both on-the-job and off-the-job training methods. On-the-job training concerns training activities conducted at a trainee's normal work setting, while off-the-job training concerns training activities conducted away from the employee's workstation. A combination of both involves training activities which may take place both at the job site and away from the workplace.

The main training techniques used for staff training involve:

Job rotation: This technique is designed to help employees acquire skills, knowledge and experience by moving them to different positions and various departments of the organization for a specified period of time. The trainees are expected to learn how each department functions within the organization (e.g. its key roles, policies, procedures) through observation and practice, as well as through instruction by a supervisor.

Coaching: This is also a one-to-one instruction in which an employee's supervisor sets a good example of what is to be done and then examines the employee's performance, offers counselling on how to maintain effective performance and corrects performance problems.

Behaviour modelling or observational learning: This is a process where the employee observes a task which is done by others (e.g. supervisors, managers, co-workers) who serve as role models and then the employee performs the observed act. Essentially, this is a process of learning from other people's experience by simulating their behaviour.

Shadowing: This is a popular technique where normally employees gain an understanding of a job in a different department by walking through the work day as a shadow to a competent worker. This allows the trainee to view first-hand the skills in practice in order to inform job choices or to develop cross-departmental understanding.

Lectures in a classroom. This is a technique where formal teaching takes place using audiovisual and static media such as video, handouts and books. A variety of views, as well as experiences can be exchanged among trainees. The emphasis in learning is usually on providing background knowledge on a specific topic. This is also a technique where trainees use and develop their knowledge and skills to solve real job-related problems involving case studies,[1] role plays,[2] in-basket exercises[3] and business games.[4]

Simulation. This is a technique where training equipment and devices are used to reproduce a real work situation in a risk-controlled learning environment, that is an environment where the consequences of 'getting it wrong' are carefully controlled. Employees develop their skills on these devices and then transfer them on the actual equipment used on the job.

Computer-based training. This technique can be used in a variety of settings and as a self-paced training method. Computer-based training may include distance learning university courses, teaching of computer literacy skills, simulations and business games. The use of computer-based training has spread rapidly in many organizations during the last years due to the fact that it offers fast learning, can be highly efficient (e.g. it can deliver exactly what the learners need, at the time when they need it and in the form that they prefer) and can allow instant feedback of results to learners.

Apprenticeship training. This is a technique which consists of classroom instruction and teaching, as well as on-the-job training. Apprenticeship training is mandatory for admission to many of the technical-skilled trades such as plumbing where the employees are required to be trained (in a classroom as well as on the job) for a specific number of hours.

Action learning. This technique is based on learning by experience. It differs from traditional management training mainly in the respect that action learning material is not books or written cases but actual organizational problems, that is real problems from the work situation for trainees to solve. Trainees are formed into a small group, they are assigned a defined project to work on and they, in turn, undertake research in order to develop a solution which can be implemented in the workplace.

As far as it concerns the decision regarding the selection of appropriate training techniques, a number of factors should be considered, such as the time and money available to design and deliver an effective training program, trainee characteristics, objectives of the training program and availability of human and physical resources. For example, a lack of well-qualified trainers or a lack of adequate training facilities may force an organization to choose on-the-job training techniques to deliver the training program (e.g. coaching) instead of using off-the-job training (e.g. simulation).

The evaluation phase

The training and development evaluation is defined as the collection of information necessary to measure how well a training and development activity met its objectives. The process of evaluation involves issues such as the objectives of training evaluation (i.e. what are the reasons for evaluating the training effort), the methods employed for collecting relevant information and the resources needed to carry out an effective evaluation. Unfortunately, many organizations do not include an evaluation phase as part of their training and development efforts due to misconceptions that undermine this stage of the training cycle, such as the perception that training evaluation adds cost to the training process (e.g. costs of materials and the down time of staff involved in the evaluation, salary of the human resource developer etc.) without offering exact results about the training activity which can be transformed into specific indicators for future action. However, evaluation is a stage that cannot be ignored, and it is very important for the success of a training and development effort.

More specifically, training and development evaluation can help to do the following:

• Determine whether a training and development program met its objectives
• Identify the strong and the weak points of a training and development program
• Determine the cost-benefit ratio of a training and development program

• Identify which participants benefited the most or least from the program
• Decide who should participate in future training and development efforts

Evaluation must be conducted before or at the start of the training program, during the training and development program and after the training program. This helps the human resource development professionals to know the level of knowledge and skills of the learners before they start the program, to evaluate the effectiveness of the program as it progresses by assessing the trainees' understanding during the event and to evaluate whether the training program met its objectives, as well as the satisfaction of the learners. Therefore, evaluation should not be considered as the final stage in the training and development process, but it should take place at all stages. The most popular model of the training evaluation process is the four-level framework developed by Donald Kirkpatrick and includes the following four criteria:

1   *Reactions.* Reactions are based on the trainee's perceptions about the program and if the person liked it, including its content, the trainer and the methods used. This can be proved useful information for the design of future training and development activities. It usually involves interviews with the trainees and filling of questionnaires in order to assess their opinions and beliefs about the program.
2   *Learning.* This is a criterion which measures how well the trainees have learned what they should have learned according to the training and development objectives of the program. It involves special tests and quizzes which measure how well the trainees have learned particular skills.
3   *Behaviour.* This criterion examines mainly the transfer of learning and training and it is very important because indicates if the trainees have improved their performance on the job as a result of their training. It involves direct observation of the trainee's behaviour on the workplace identifying changes in skills and abilities.
4   *Results.* This criterion measures if the training and development effort improved the organization's effectiveness. It involves a cost-benefit analysis by providing data and information on the cost of training, staff productivity, sales, absenteeism, staff turnover, rate of errors, rate of accidents and product/service quality before and after the training intervention.

Creating a learning organization

A learning organization is called an *organization where the focus is on the acquisition, sharing and utilization of knowledge to survive and prosper.* In such organizations, learning is supported, facilitated and rewarded by line managers. It is imperative in the turbulent business environment that most organizations operate to evolve into learning organizations because their survival and success depends heavily on investment in skills. Line managers need to know about the key features of a learning organization so that they can work towards creating the conditions to encourage organizational learning. Specifically, line managers should adhere to the following steps in order to encourage learning at work:

- They should adopt a learning approach to strategy. This means that HR and line managers should have the authority to make small operational changes, which they treat subsequently as experiments.
- They should adopt a participative policymaking, that is taking into account the views of all stakeholders and especially their own staff. This may lead to the adoption of innovative approaches towards staff learning.
- They should create formative control and reporting systems to assist learning. This will give information to managers on the areas in which employees need further development.
- They should develop a range of rewards to employees (both financial and non-financial) for exchange of ideas and knowledge and for the application of new skills.
- They should design jobs in such a way that enhance workplace learning. For example, the creation of *communities of practice* where employees with a common interest in a particular domain work in the same location and exchange knowledge and ideas, as well as the encouragement of team-working and task variety are some ways where individual learning could be stimulated.
- They should create effective IT systems to capture staff knowledge and provide information for all (e.g. creation of expert directories where each employee can share job-related information and knowledge on the company's intranet).
- They should introduce job swaps and develop frequent training interventions to expand employee skills.
- They should not blame employees for making simple mistakes. Instead, they should encourage staff to reflect on their behaviour, question ideas and actions, value mistakes as learning opportunities and evaluate staff learning.
- They should develop performance appraisal mechanisms that encourage staff to give feedback on managers' actions. This will help the organization to improve the quality of managerial supervision (including their coaching skills).

Notes

1 Trainees use problem-solving skills to find solutions to work-related situations which are presented in stories (cases).

2 Trainees are presented with an organizational situation, act out a particular role in the situation and then review the implications of their behaviour.

3 Trainees are asked to organize, prioritize, plan and make decisions within a specified time regarding a number of issues and documents (reports, notes, letters, memos) typically found in a manager's desk.

4 Trainees must make decisions about various organizational situations and problems under strict time constraints and pressure.

8 People rewards

The purpose of this chapter is to look at the concept of strategic motivation. Employee motivation will be critically discussed along with its implications for people management. The chapter further aims to explain the components of a systematic compensation program and discuss how organizations can link pay to performance.

Human motivation

The study of motivation is concerned, basically, with why people behave in a certain way. The basic underlying question is 'Why do people do what they do?'. In general terms, motivation can be described as the direction and persistence of action. It is actually an internal state that energizes human behaviour. It is concerned with why people choose a particular course of action in preference to others, and why they continue with a chosen action, often over a long period, and in the face of difficulties and problems. With a positive motivation philosophy and practice in place, productivity, quality and service should improve because motivation helps people towards achieving goals; gaining a positive perspective; creating the power to change; building self-esteem and capability; and managing their development and helping others.

Employee motivation is one of the most challenging aspects of HRM. It manifests itself through employee morale, output, absenteeism and so on. Generally, managers do not understand motivation, and its essence remains largely enigmatic. However, in the following sections a conscious effort will be made to analyze what actually motivates individuals at work.

Factors affecting motivation at work

Several theories of motivation have attempted to explain motivation in terms of factors that initiate employee behaviour. The most popular of them is Maslow's needs hierarchy theory. The particular theory argues that employees are motivated to satisfy five basic types of needs that are arranged in hierarchy of importance (i.e. physiological needs such as food and water; safety needs such as job security; social needs such as friendship; esteem needs that include job status and recognition; self-actualization needs, which involves the realization of potential through interesting and challenging work, participation in decision-making etc.), with lower order needs (i.e. physiological and safety) requiring satisfaction before the next higher order need can motivate behaviour.

Many other theories have attempted to explain motivation in terms of the thought processes that employees go through in choosing their behaviour such as the expectancy theory by Vroom. The basis of the expectancy model is that motivation is a function of the desirability of the outcome of behaviour. In other words, if an individual believes that behaving in a particular way will generate rewards that the individual values and seeks, the person will be motivated to produce those behaviours.

In short, managers need to know that the main factors affecting individual motivation at work are: employee perception; values; personal needs; personality characteristics; innate and acquired abilities; work environment (e.g. job design, firm culture, employee relations with colleagues and managers etc.); rewards (financial and non-financial); and the external environment (e.g. economic pressures, change in regulations etc.). Rewards can be either intrinsic (i.e. those rewards that accrue to the individual as a direct result of the job itself), such as providing the employees with a great variety of tasks, or/and extrinsic (such rewards are generated from outside the job itself), such as bonus schemes. The key factor in intrinsic satisfaction is finding a job which uses the talents one has. Several surveys around employee satisfaction place the nature of the work itself among the most important variables affecting motivation along with job security and pay.

At a more practical level, what is important for managers to understand is that motivation is an individual-level phenomenon that allows for the existence of cognitive processes (see also Chapter 3). Therefore, managers need to be aware of individual employee needs, ensure that rewards are tied to performance and ensure that rewards satisfy needs which are important to employees. Managers also need to understand that although money is regarded as the most important single motivator, yet it is not the sole one.

In order to enhance employee performance, managers need to take into account some key variables affecting job satisfaction, such as skills variety, task identity, task significance, autonomy, feedback and employee growth need strength (i.e. individual differences in the desire for personal growth). It has been shown in several research studies that those jobs that score high on the preceding characteristics have the potential to bring high internal motivation to employees, thus leading to low turnover and absenteeism, as well as improved performance.

The degree to which employees are willing to exert effort and commit to organizational goals is dependent on two basic conditions:

1 The extent to which employee expectations of what the organization will give them and what they owe the organization in return matches the organization's expectations of what it will give and receive
2 Assuming there is agreement on these expectations, the specific nature of what is exchanged (e.g. effort for pay)

These mutual expectations constitute part of the 'psychological contract', which is an unwritten agreement between the employee and the organization that specifies what each part expects to give and receive from the other. These implicit agreements that do not involve formal aspects of the employment relationship, such as pay, and that normally focus on challenging work, fair treatment, opportunity for creativity and so on may be more important than written agreements for enhancing work motivation. Therefore, managing the psychological contract successfully can be one of the most challenging aspects of HR and line managers' jobs. The more attuned the manager is to the needs and expectations of subordinates, the greater the number of matches that are likely to exist in the psychological contract.

Types of rewards and different compensation systems

The main compensation objectives for the employees are two: to satisfy their individual needs and to ensure equitable treatment. On the other hand, the main compensation objectives for the organization are the following: to attract and keep the desired quality of workers; to motivate the workforce; to reinforce the desired corporate culture (by rewarding those employees who support the core organizational values); to control the labour costs; and to comply with legal requirements

This section identifies and discusses developments in employee reward and considers the practical ways in which reward management can be used, as part of various HR practices, to elicit employee engagement and drive individual and organizational performance. The subject of reward is vast and continually evolving. It has been described by several authors as a bundle of monetary and non-monetary returns offered in exchange for a number of employee contributions. It is widely recognized that the most effective approaches to reward are based on careful consideration of an underlying philosophy and strategy that corresponds to the overall business strategy. In accordance with this belief, it follows that organizations should ensure that rewards are linked to the firm's values and beliefs and support the wider corporate objectives. Whilst accepting the notion of aligning reward to business strategy to optimize the utility of reward mechanisms, a number of key choices must be made in the process. In particular, there are four basic reward decisions a company needs to draw consensus on:

- What to pay for (i.e. job size, performance, skills/qualifications, personal attributes)
- Whether to place primary focus on internal equity or be more concerned with external benchmarks
- Whether to operate a centralized or decentralized approach or even a hybrid approach to reward
- Whether to build hierarchy into the reward system or to devise a single-status approach

Employees can be paid for the time they work, the output they produce, skills and experience or a combination of these factors. The main methods of payment include (a) flat rates where employees get a specific amount of money per hour regardless of seniority or performance and (b) variable pay, which involves any compensation plan that emphasizes a shared focus on organizational success and operates outside the base pay increase system. This may include skill-based pay and performance-related pay. Among the main factors affecting rewards for each job are job evaluation, firm profitability, labour laws (e.g. regulations on National Minimum Wage, or NMW), market posture of the organization, existence and power of trade unions and the wider economic climate.

The compensation process should start with an accurate job description so that a proper 'job evaluation' could be conducted. The 'job evaluation' is a systematic method of determining the worth to the organization of a job in relation to the worth of other jobs. The criteria used to determine the 'value' of a job are numerous, ranging from physical working conditions and level of education to mental and physical effort. The main job evaluation systems include job ranking, job grading and point system. The point system, which is quite popular, involves quantifying a set of job factors such as education, experience, responsibility, working conditions and so on by allocating points to each factor. An example of a point system is given in Table 8.1.

As soon as the process of job evaluation finishes, then the relevant specific rewards to be given to employees should be determined. The main types of employee rewards can be divided in two broad categories: financial and non-financial rewards (Table 8.2). Managers need to use a mix of rewards so that employees can satisfy their different needs.

Table 8.1 Example of a point system

Job factor: education	Level	Points
PhD degree	4	400
Master's degree	3	300
Bachelor degree	2	200
Secondary education	1	100

Table 8.2 Types of rewards

Financial rewards	Non-financial rewards
Wages, bonuses, commissions, insurance (life, medical), pension schemes, holiday packages, childcare, employee loans, employee discounts in products/services, paid transportation, gym membership, free parking, company car, profit sharing	Flexible work schedules, interesting and challenging work, job autonomy, career advancement, training, safe and healthy environment, friendly colleagues, competent and supportive supervisor, fair treatment

Bonus and incentives

Two of the most popular types of compensation plans involve bonus and incentives. A bonus is a discretionary reward provided by managers after a successful employee performance. It may be awarded for a well-defined accomplishment, or it may simply be given to recognize extra effort. A bonus is awarded after the job is done, and it makes no guarantee that future effort will be rewarded similarly. By contrast, an incentive is a proactive reward plan. Its aim is to direct an employee's behaviour by establishing performance objectives and rewarding the achievement of these objectives. An incentive system is more likely to result in improved employee performance because it clarifies job expectations and directly links pay to performance. For example, the use of a commission on sales revenue is a typical incentive pay system for sales representatives.

Although incentive plans may have some disadvantages (e.g. in the case of individual incentive plans, they may encourage individualism and non-productive competition), they can have a significant impact on key performance indicators if they are well-designed. Some key principles that managers should follow to create effective incentive plans are:

- Development of clear goals. The plan should be simple to understand by employees and should be based on measurable performance objectives.
- Identification of the source of funding. A well-designed incentive plan will fund its payments from the relevant increases in staff productivity.

- Constructive feedback to employees around their progress.
- Frequent rewards. The best plans pay employees frequently.
- Pay for performance. The best plans emphasize the link between performance and reward.

Job re-design

One of the ways that employee performance could be improved and is frequently ignored by managers is through job design. Effective job design can empower employees by increasing the levels of employee participation and self-determination at work. The most popular techniques of job design that have the potential to empower employees are:

- *Job enrichment.* This involves an increase of job variety. Employees are given various tasks to perform that usually make their job more interesting and enable them to develop a range of skills.
- *Job rotation.* Employees are given the opportunity to move between different departments for a certain period of time in order to gain different skills, as well as develop their network.
- *Quality circles.* This involves a technique where a team of employees performing similar jobs meets regularly during work times to discuss various work-related problems (e.g. issues around product quality, production problems etc.). Members are trained in problem-solving techniques and present their solutions to management formally. The underlying logic behind quality circles is that employees are likely to accept any organizational changes more easily when they are the source of suggested changes.
- *Self-directed work teams.* This is a technique where a highly trained group of employees is given full responsibility to create a specific product or undertake a specific work-related project. Team members are trained to perform a variety of cross-functional tasks. With this technique, the need for formal managerial supervision is eliminated. Workers schedule their own work, which results in increased job satisfaction.

It should be emphasized that the preceding techniques come with certain limitations. For example, it is difficult for managers to create self-management teams using a team of low-skilled workers. Also, when companies are using quality circles they need to ensure that the lost working time spent on meetings results in real added value for the organization. Despite the aforementioned limitations, evidence shows that they can be important variables affecting staff motivation.

Work-life balance

Work-life balance (WLB) practices are also considered to be a powerful reward for many employees and have been shown to reduce staff absence, raise employee morale and increase job satisfaction. It has been argued by several commentators in the HRM literature that there can be several barriers and problems with work-life balance practices, such as the nature of some jobs (e.g. some jobs are not doable on anything less than a full-time basis), meeting team performance targets, difficulty in managing employee careers, limited transmission of tacit knowledge. Despite such concerns, work-life balance practices can offer significant organizational benefits including higher staff productivity and reduced costs associated with the poor health of employees. Whether or not there is a work-life balance policy in existence, it is often line managers who will be the main actors in transforming WLB policies into reality by their attitudes. Some of the most popular options for achieving WLB are part-time work; flexitime; compressed week; term-time working; job share; shift swapping; unpaid leave; and work from home.

Rewards and staff retention

People leave jobs for a variety of different reasons, some of which are wholly outside the power of the company to influence (e.g. retirement). In many cases, people leave for a mixture of reasons, certain factors weighting more highly in their minds than others, but all are related to the broader concept of rewards. The following two major categories of factors may explain the reasons people voluntarily leaving a job:

1   Push factors (dissatisfaction with work itself or the organization): Such factors include limited training and development provision, boring tasks, ineffective supervision, poor levels of employee involvement in decision-making, poor financial rewards and so on.
2   Pull factors (employee 'poaching' by other employers): Such factors include better training and development opportunities provided by competitors, more job autonomy, higher rewards and so on.

Most research studies have concluded that push factors are more prevalent than pull factors as causes of voluntary resignations. It seems that very few employees are willing to leave jobs in which they are broadly happy in search of something even better. Instead the picture is one in which dissatisfied employees seek alternatives because they no longer enjoy working for their present employer. The key message for HR and line managers is that they can readily address all of these issues that lead employees to resign by providing them with a better deal in the broadest sense. The main reason that so many managers fail to do so is the absence of mechanisms for picking up signs of dissatisfaction (e.g. no opportunity to voice concerns/poor communication). All the practices of effective people management described in this book can play a significant part in reducing staff turnover.

9 The employment relationship

The key purpose of this chapter is to present the main tools that managers can use to create a harmonious working environment. Contemporary forms of job design and work organization will be explored along with their impact on the employment relationship. Other important thematic areas such as discipline, grievances and occupational health and safety are also examined.

Nature of the employment relationship

In broad terms, employment relations is concerned with the theory and practice associated with the management and regulation of the employment relationship. Specifically, it is concerned with the sociopolitical dimensions of the employment relationship and the distribution of power between management and employees, the incidence and expression of conflict and the social and legislative regulatory framework within which the employment relationship exists. On a theoretical level, there are three main perspectives of the relationship between capital and labour that reflect different views of the balance of power and the legitimacy of worker resistance to managerial action. These are the *unitarist* approach; the *pluralist* approach; and the *Marxist* approach. Unitarism views organizations as unified entities where all parties have common objectives, conflict is irrational and the employment relationship is essentially consensual. Pluralism views organizations as entities comprising a coalition of different groups with diverse interests where conflict is unavoidable and power relations are fluid. Industrial action under the guidance of trade unions is considered a legitimate expression of conflict. Last, Marxism views the relationship between capital and labour based on class conflict, stating that there is a fundamental imbalance of power.

It becomes evident that unitarism is closely linked to the theory of strategic HRM. In this context, the employment relationship is individualized and trade unions are seen as unwelcome; instead, the link between HRM and employee relations is developed through the psychological contract. However, the new realism in the domain of employee relations is a focus on developing and implementing strategic HRM in a context where unions have a role to play in the workplace and as such a collective approach is required. The approach mostly commonly adopted in this context is the establishment of a partnership agreement between the employer and the union. High-commitment HR practices and trade unions are not considered to be mutually exclusive, and in some circumstances union presence can contribute to the achievement of the goals of HRM, such as employee commitment, flexibility and quality.

As mentioned previously, the psychological contract looks at the reality of the employment situation as perceived by the parties and may be more influential than the formal contract in affecting how employees behave from day to day. It is the psychological contract that effectively tells employees what they are required to do in order to meet their side of the bargain and what they can expect from their job. Against this background, the 'new' psychological contract states that among the main employer's responsibilities are high pay for high job performance, opportunities for self-development and employability driven by changes in this and future employment. On the other hand, employees' key responsibilities include the application at work of a range of knowledge and skills, and making a difference to the organization.

Discipline and grievances

Discipline is regulation of human activity to produce a controlled performance. However, it should be stressed to all managers that disciplinary procedures should not be viewed primarily as a means of imposing sanctions to employees but as a way of helping and encouraging improvement amongst employees whose conduct or standard of work is unsatisfactory. Discipline is, therefore, not only negative, producing punishment, but also a valuable quality for the individual who is subject to it (self-discipline). Managers should not deal with discipline only when rebuking latecomers. As well as dealing with the unruly and reluctant, they should be developing the coordinated discipline of the working team, and they should be training the new recruits who must not let down the rest of the team.

There are some specific stages that managers should follow to discipline employees effectively. These are the following:

• Managers should make sure that they know all the facts and have all the evidence needed before 'accusing' an employee of misbehaviour. It may damage an employee's motivation and trust towards the senior management team if an employee faces an unfair accusation.

- Managers should arrange a personal meeting with the employee they wish to discipline. The meeting should be arranged at the earliest opportunity. The immediate action helps employees to understand the close link that exists between their particular action and the penalty associated with that kind of behaviour. Moreover, it is crucial for the manager to conduct the meeting in private. Managers should not forget that employees wish to be praised in public but be punished in private. So, it is important for managers to protect employee morale in such situations.
- Managers should give employees the opportunity to explain the reasons underlying their behaviour. An employee may have a profound reason for his or her misbehaviour (e.g. caring responsibilities of a sick family member that creates problems of punctuality at work). Managers should listen carefully to their staff in order to take the right course of action.
- Last but not least, managers need to ensure that the penalty imposed reflects the severity of the case/event (e.g. it would not be reasonable to fire an employee for being half an hour late at his work if this happened once a year).

Regarding grievances, we will include in this term not only the complaints that have been formally presented to an appropriate management representative or to a union official but also the spoken or written dissatisfaction of employees brought to the attention of a manager. Grievances can be rare since few employees wish to question their superior's judgement and fewer risk being stigmatized as a troublemaker. Also, many employees do not initiate grievances because they believe that nothing will be done as a result of their attempt. However, HR and line managers have to encourage the proper use of procedures to discover sources of dissatisfaction among their staff because the dissatisfaction lying beneath a repressed grievance can produce unsatisfactory work behaviours (e.g. apathy). The key features that grievance procedures should have in small and large organizations are fairness to avoid the risk of inconsistent decisions; certain procedural steps (e.g. preliminary step where the manager attempts to satisfy the employee and next steps if the employee wants to take the issue further); and promptness to avoid employee frustration that can come from severe delay.

Following are some basic guidelines that can guide HR and line managers towards creating a harmonious working environment:

- Increase employee engagement in decision-making. Employees feel bonded to the organization, and more motivated, if they participate in various business decisions. Managers may adopt in several cases a more democratic managerial style that allows more employee involvement in job design, training and so on.

- Be a coach for your employees. In an era where job security is almost an unknown word, most employees look at improving their knowledge base and develop their skills so that they can remain employable in the job market. Managers need to understand that informal learning is precious for workers and in certain cases a stronger motivator than money.
- Spend quality time with your employees and listen to their concerns and ideas not only during the working time but also during various other occasions such as office luncheons, training seminars, staff nights out and so on.
- Be fair. Nothing creates discontent in the workplace faster than obvious favouritism towards certain employees. Enforce rules uniformly and reward high performance and exceeded expectations the same way for every employee.
- Resolve interpersonal conflicts effectively as discussed in Chapter 4. This means that the manager should ensure that strong emotions are not aroused among employees. Differences in views are quite frequently essential to change. Besides, if there was no need for disagreement, the organization would probably be in a state of apathy. However, excessive conflict can produce destructive behaviour, and hence, HR and line managers should aim to achieve positive outcomes from any conflict.

Employee involvement initiatives

Employee involvement (EI) seeks to harness the talents of employees through the soliciting of their views, opinions and ideas to identify and address organizational problems. In practice, EI is often focused on the engagement of small groups and individuals in addressing local, operational issues by facilitating information-sharing within work groups and between line managers and employees. Generally, EI does not extend to providing the opportunity for workers to have an input into higher-level, strategic decision-making, such as pay, working conditions or wider organizational policy. Examples of involvement mechanisms include quality circles, teamworking and self-managed work groups, which were discussed in Chapter 6.

Employee participation (EP) is regarded as a more substantial form of voice than EI because it tends to incorporate a greater degree of joint decision-making between management and employees. EP results from a desire among employees to have greater influence over decisions that directly or indirectly affect them. Because participation is often concerned with negotiation, conflict may occur between employees and management.

However, EP can also help to channel conflict to more effective resolution. In practice, EP is implemented through works councils and joint consultative committees.

Managing workplace health and safety

The topic of health and safety at work is a very important area of the employment relationship. Unfortunately, health and safety is regarded as a marginal issue by many managers. However, lack of training and resources in the area of occupational health and safety can cause several problems to organizations, including absenteeism, cost (e.g. medical compensation to workers) and increased staff turnover. The importance of management commitment cannot be overstated. The provision of a safe working environment requires more than reducing the number of workplace accidents. Managers have to deal with various issues and develop formal policies around sexual harassment, smoking and substance abuse, violence at work, work-family conflict, AIDS and so on. Organizations have ethical, legal and business obligations to provide their employees with a safe environment. Failure to do so is simply bad management. It should become clear that occupational health should be part of every manager's job and not just the responsibility of the HR manager. The main elements of a successful health and safety strategy include the firm's culture and systems of health and safety. Without a culture that values the well-being of everyone at work, there will always be human victims. In terms of systems, there should be adequate employee induction on safety at work, continuous staff training, policies, standards and audits.

10 Organizational change

This chapter will look at the nature of changes that normally take place in organizations of various sizes and will further examine how this process can be managed effectively through people management.

Nature of organizational change

All managers are now familiar with the argument that change is a constant in the business world and that its pace is increasing. Inevitably, therefore, managers will find themselves leading, promoting, encouraging and stimulating change as a key part of their role. There is a good deal of literature identifying the drivers for change such as competitor behaviour, customer expectations, technological advancements and so on. However, underlying all of this is the fundamental reason for change, which is organizational survival and competitiveness in the complex and global world of business.

The nature of change has also been hotly debated, and the emphasis has been on transformational change. Change can be either proactive or reactive to an unexpected event, operational (e.g. introducing new machinery) or strategic (e.g. entering new markets) and may involve movements in organizational size, structure, rewards, values, systems, procedures, tasks and behaviour. Whilst transformational change may involve all of these, it is generally agreed that it is more than this and involves fundamentally new ways of understanding what the organization is for and is doing. All change, no matter how small, presents a challenge to HR and line managers because making a change is not just a 'technical' matter but essentially a human one.

The process of change

There is a variety of models in the literature which suggests several stages that managers should follow in order to implement changes effectively. Most models focus on four main stages:

1   *Identify the need for change.* In this initial stage, managers are required to identify any performance gaps, generate scenarios for anticipated changes in the internal and external environment of the organization and vision the future desired state. During this stage, managers review the planned strategic objectives and monitor the actual organizational performance to see if the organization met its goals. At this stage, several quantitative and qualitative indices are reviewed (e.g. productivity, sales, turnover, customer satisfaction etc.) to evaluate if there is any significant deviance from the initially planned objectives. Furthermore, an extensive analysis is undertaken on the external and internal forces acting on organizations that may act as drivers for change.

2   *Diagnose capacity for change.* In this stage, managers should attempt to identify barriers to change and examine how they can be overcome. For example, a common barrier to organizational change is employee resistance, which is normally caused by the fear of the unknown, fear of financial loss, threat to job security and existing status and loss of job autonomy.

3   *Implement required action.* In this stage, managers should choose proper interventions to facilitate organizational changes. It is the stage where managers should provide a strong motive for change and help employees abandon old behaviours and adopt new ones. This stage normally involves (a) formal staff meetings to inform the staff about the nature of change, reasons for change and impact of change on their jobs in order to reduce their fear of the unknown; (b) staff training to enable employees to develop the new gamut of skills that may be required by the organizational changes; (c) employee participation and involvement in change to feel that they are actively involved and go along with it; and (d) provision of rewards (either monetary or non-monetary) to encourage employees to support actively the proposed changes. For example, the provision of a flexible work schedule in return for changing work patterns.

4   *Measure progress.* In this final change, managers need to monitor key performance indicators such as productivity, sales, rate of errors, absenteeism, customer complaints, faulty products and so on before and after change to determine if the change had indeed a positive impact on the overall organizational performance.

Managers need to be aware of the crucial role of 'emotions' in the implementation of change since change is usually exhilarating when done *by* us and disturbing when done *to* us. This means that employee resistance to change is a characteristic of the individual human psyche that, ultimately, has to be overcome rather than that resistance stems from legitimate reasons and is partly a result of the way that change is conceived and led in the organization. In this context, effective communication, training and negotiation through the provision of rewards are important elements of managing change. The major challenge for managers is to gain employee commitment during organizational changes instead of forcing through the proposed change by virtue of the power. This requires managers to get to the heart of employee concerns. Although there are cases where a coercion strategy might look a desirable approach to implement change, especially when speed to organizational change is crucial (e.g. during a sudden financial crisis), still it can be risky in the long term because it will normally leave employees mad at the initiators, and if people feel manipulated, they may leave the organization as soon as alternative employment becomes available.

11 Managing employee stress

Given the complex nature of businesses, people who work in them are frequently subject to a range of pressures, some of which may lead to individual stress. This chapter looks at the nature of stress and its causes and describes some of the actions that can be taken by organizations and individuals to reduce stress.

Definition and causes of occupational stress

Stress is simply defined as a condition where a consequence of events place high levels of physical and psychological demand on individuals. Stress is more than mere pressure (which can be considered 'stimulating' stress) and leads to breakdown of human performance. Important examples of specific factors that have been found to contribute to stress concern the external environment (economic situation, political changes); the organization itself (management style, rewards, work relationships, job characteristics); and the personal situation (personality type, home and social life). The symptoms of stress are typically physiological (indigestion, high blood pressure, back pain), psychological (obsessions, phobias, depression) and behavioural (smoking, alcohol consumption, aggression, insomnia).

There are a number of reasons why managers should take a strong interest in managing occupational stress within their organizations. Some of them include improved performance through the reduction of errors in production/customer service, higher productivity, cost reduction (caused from employee absences, staff turnover, accidents) and improved brand image (caused by the improved ethical stance of the organization towards its staff).

Dealing with occupational stress

The coping strategies can be divided in two main categories and are presented in Table 11.1.

Table 11.1 Coping mechanisms for work-related stress

Personal strategies	Organizational strategies
– Relaxation techniques (e.g. yoga, physical exercise) – Network development to encourage communication (e.g. sharing of feelings among colleagues) – Healthy diet to minimize the emergence of stress owing to physiological causes – Improved time management to reduce the stress caused by an increasing workload – Behaviour control (individuals learn to recognize their own behaviour and practice cognitive techniques to cope with stressful situations)	– Professional counselling provision to staff (e.g. cognitive behavioural therapy provided by trained therapists) – Stress management and conflict management training seminars to raise employee awareness – Job re-design to reduce employee workload and increase job satisfaction through increased autonomy and task significance – Increased employee involvement in decision-making and improved communication processes – Improved HR policies (i.e. employee friendly) such as flexible working arrangements that can help work-life balance

Regarding the organizational interventions, it should be pointed out that there is nothing outstanding about the measures in Table 11.1, which are likely to be seen in a well-managed company that views its employees as its most valuable asset, as well as one of its main stakeholders. As for the individual measures, two of the most popular techniques that employees can use to reduce their anxiety include (a) communicating with others and obtaining social support and (b) practicing the ABCDE technique developed by the psychologist Albert Ellis, which involves the following steps:

A (activating agent): identify the stressor
B (belief system): identify rational and irrational beliefs
C (consequences): identify the mental, physical and behavioural consequences
D (dispute irrational beliefs): challenge your initial beliefs by findings new references to support your new thoughts. Through selective awareness and self-talk, you can remove cognitive distortions such as over-generalizing and relabel any negative experience as a positive one.
E (effects of cognitive restructuring): measure the effects of changing your interpretation of a situation. Ideally you can now take practical action to solve the problem or have a less troublesome reaction to the situation.

12 Organizational communication

The importance of interpersonal communication for organizational effectiveness cannot be overstated. As it was stressed in previous chapters, communication is the glue that holds organizations together. Against this background, the final chapter examines how communication between managers and employees can be improved.

The process of communication

Communication assists organizational members to accomplish both individual and organizational goals, as well as implement various organizational changes. The key question to be asked around organizational communication is whether managers will communicate well or poorly with their staff. The general process of communication involves five core elements: *the communicator* (who sends a message), *the message* (content of information), *the medium* (the way the content is transmitted), *the receiver* (the person who gets the information) and *feedback* (the effect of information provided). Two of the most important stages that take place in this process are the encoding and decoding stages. The encoding translates the communicator's ideas into a systematic set of symbols, whereas decoding involves interpretation by the receiver in light of his or her own previous experiences and frames of reference. This underscores the importance of the communicator being 'receiver-oriented'.

There are several barriers to effective communication, including different frames of reference (different individuals may interpret the same message differently depending on their previous experiences); selective listening (individuals tend to block out new information, especially if it conflicts with what they believe); source credibility (the level of credibility the receiver assigns to the communicator); and time pressures (in their effort to meet strict deadlines managers may give messages to employees partially).

Improving organizational communication

Some of the basic steps that managers should follow in improving communication in organizations are discussed next:

Following up. This involves assuming that you are misunderstood and you attempt to determine whether your intended meaning was received.

Regulating information flow. Communication is regulated in terms of both quality and quantity. For example, only significant deviations from policies and procedures should be brought to the attention of superiors.

Utilizing feedback. Feedback is important to ensure that the message has been received by employees and has produced the intended response.

Empathy. This involves being receiver-oriented rather than communicator-oriented. Empathy requires communicators to place themselves in the position of the receiver in order to anticipate and understand how the message is likely to be decoded by the receiver. The greater the gap between the experiences and background of the communicator and the receiver, the greater is the effort that must be made to find a common ground of understanding.

Repetition. Repetition in communication can ensure that if one part of the message is not understood, other parts will carry the same message. For example, managers should provide the newcomers to the organization with the same basic information in several different forms.

Simplifying language. Managers must encode messages in words and symbols that are meaningful to the receiver. They should not use technical jargon that transforms simple concepts into complex puzzles because they need to remember that effective communication involves transmitting information, as well as understanding. If the receiver does not understand, then there has been no communication.

Effective listening. To improve communication managers must seek to be understood but also to understand, which involves effective listening. Removing distractions, putting the speaker at ease, summarizing an explanation given by the speaker, showing the speaker you want to listen and asking questions all contribute to good listening. Managers need to understand the importance of their decision to listen, which lies in the fact that it can encourage their subordinates to express their true feelings and desires.

Interpersonal styles and emotional intelligence of managers

The daily activities of managers place a high value on effective communications. Managers provide information (which must be understood), they give instructions (which must be followed) and they attempt to influence staff to accept various organizational rules. The way in which managers communicate is crucial for obtaining effective performance. There are several different managerial styles when it comes to interpersonal communication ranging from autocratic leaders who show coldness towards others to more democratic ones who value the views of others but are unable to open up and express their own feelings. However, the most effective interpersonal communication style identified in the literature is the one that uses a balance of exposure (i.e. the process that the self uses to increase the information known to others) and feedback (i.e. the individual's willingness to hear the feedback from others). Managers who are secure in their positions will feel free to expose their own feelings and to obtain feedback from others.

Effective communication implies that HR and line managers will have to develop their 'emotional intelligence', which is essential for success at work. As recent studies have revealed, emotional intelligence can be more important than intellectual intelligence when it comes to managing employees effectively. Emotional intelligence is defined as the ability to understand and manage both your own emotions and those of the people around you. In this context, managers need to have a clear picture on their strengths and weaknesses, recognize their values, learn how to put themselves in someone else's position and practice responding both to their own and employee feelings.

13 Measuring the impact of people management on organizational performance

In this final chapter, an important topic is discussed concerning the evaluation of HR effectiveness. The chapter essentially highlights for HR and lines managers the importance of measuring and communicating the contribution of people management in organizational success and describes approaches used in evaluating its impact on profits.

Importance of HR audit

Effective people management means that its impact on organizational success should be clear to all shareholders. The view that HR contributions are solely intangible and cannot be measured, which is hugely supported by too many personnel professionals, has resulted in HR function getting less status and influence in many organizations. Many line managers also support the idea that certain people-related activities are luxuries that organizations cannot afford during tough economic times. Such assumptions undermine the role of the HR function and require personnel specialists to start pointing out its impact on firm profitability. Organizations live and die by the bottom line, so it is crucial for a function to show in economic terms how it adds to the bottom line. Furthermore, measuring the impact of people management on firm performance is crucial for its improvement since you cannot improve a management activity unless you can measure it.

Personnel specialists need to ensure that their function facilitates the achievement of the firm's strategic objectives and that performance is expressed not only in qualitative terms but also in quantifiable terms using facts and figures. Only then they will be able to prove that people-related activities are not among the expense items, but they have a substantial positive effect on organizational performance.

Indicators to measure HR effectiveness

People management professionals and line managers should know that the contribution of HRM to the achievement of organizational strategic objectives can be evaluated using various criteria, including staff commitment, labour competence, cost-effectiveness of labour employed, staff motivation, job satisfaction, adaptability, performance and trust. A number of quantitative and qualitative indices can be used to measure the preceding variables, including the following: the extent of labour surplus/shortage (e.g. are there any employees that are not being fully utilized?); recruitment cost data, hiring rate, time efficiency of the hiring process, quality of hiring and accuracy of job descriptions; staff productivity; the absence percentage rate (i.e. attendance records); number of customer grievances; extent of formal training provision (i.e. number of formal training days); cost of training activity; accident records; quality control records; staff turnover index; benefits costs; wage-survey records; employee grievance records; and employee satisfaction surveys.

Concluding comments

Seen in purely economic terms (i.e. from an *instrumental* perspective), employees are the human resources that contribute along with the financial and technological resources to meet the demands of all the organization's principal stakeholders. Since line managers have the responsibility for the efficient delivery of the organization's goods and services, they are fully concerned with managing all the resources available to them. In that sense, all the personnel aspects merit the term 'human resource management'. However, if the management of people is approached from a *humanistic* perspective, then the term 'people management' is more appropriate on the grounds that employed people form the focus of the all the people-related activities rather than the concept of people as resources.

One of the core arguments of this book is that the contemporary management of employees should be approached from the latter perspective (i.e. humanistic) and should be concerned with such matters as the motivation and development of the members of the organization and with their fair treatment, as well as with their general efficiency and effectiveness in producing goods and providing services. Effective people management of the 21st century means that ethical concepts such as dignity, respect and fairness should be included in the behaviour of management.

Bibliography

Adams, J. (2007) *Managing People in Organizations: Contemporary Theory and Practice*. Basingstoke: Palgrave.

Beardwell, J. and T. Claydon (2010) *Human Resource Management: A Contemporary Approach*. 6th ed. Essex: Pearson Education.

Boxall, P. and J. Purcell (2011) *Strategy and Human Resource Management*. 3rd ed. Basingstoke: Palgrave.

Cole, G. (1995) *Organizational Behaviour*. London: Letts Educational.

Harrison, R. (2005) *Learning and Development*. 4th ed. London: CIPD.

Martin, J. (2001) *Organizational Behaviour*. 2nd ed. Boston: Thomson.

Stone, R. (2002) *Human Resource Management*. 4th ed. Milton, QLD: Wiley.

Torrington, D. and L. Hall (1998) *Human Resource Management*. 4th ed. London: Prentice Hall.

Ulrich, D. (1996) *Human Resource Champions*. Cambridge, MA: Harvard Business Review Press.

Whittington, R. (1993) *What Is Strategy and Does It Matter?* London: Routledge.

Index

Page numbers for tables are in *italics*.

Printed in the United States
by Baker & Taylor Publisher Services